CYCLIC ANALYSIS:

The Dynamic New Approach
To Technical Analysis
Of Stocks and Commodities

J. M. Hurst

Traders Press, Inc.®
PO Box 6206
Greenville, SC 20606

Published by Traders Press, Inc.

The material contained herein is not to be taken as advice to buy or to sell specific securities. The information presented is based on sources we believe to be reliable and has been carefully checked for completeness and accuracy but cannot be guaranteed.

1975-2000
25th Anniversary
Traders Press Inc.
PO Box 6206
Greenville, SC 29606

800-927-8222
864-298-0222
FAX 864-298-0221
Tradersprs@aol.com
http://www.TradersPress.com

$\mathcal{P}$ublisher's Comments

For many years I had heard that the work of J.M. Hurst was of great value to technical analysts, especially those interested in the cyclical analysis of stock price movements. Upon looking into what composed the body of his work, I learned that most of it was unavailable to traders and investors. Hurst's primary work, *The Profit Magic of Stock Transaction Timing* had gone out of print. I had heard rumors that Hurst had also authored a lengthy trading course on cycles, but it, too, was long out of print. Having been involved in technical analysis and trading for many years myself, I felt that it would be a valuable contribution to the field of technical analysis to assure that the work of Hurst was "kept alive" for present and future generations of traders and analysts. I decided to make a special project of "resuscitating" his research in its various forms.

My first step was to negotiate with Prentice Hall for the rights to reprint *Profit Magic* as a Traders Press publication. This done, I next set about to locate a copy of the Hurst course. I knew that Hurst himself would be the best source of information on it. However, due to the various rumors I had heard about Hurst, I assumed that he was no longer living. No one had seen or heard from him in many years and it was commonly rumored that he had died. I conducted a search to find not only the Hurst course, but also to determine whether Hurst was still living and if so, how to contact him. Months of diligent searching finally turned up a copy of the course. Jim Tillman, a cycles analyst of considerable repute, owned a copy of the course and was kind enough to let me use it in order to reproduce the course. A further search for the owner of the rights to the course proved successful, and I purchased them from him. A final search resulted in finding Hurst alive and well, to my surprise and delight. I have since had a very pleasant association and friendship with him. He has asked me to keep his location and contact information confidential, and I intend to respect that wish.

After reprinting *Profit Magic* and the Hurst Cycles Course, and sending copies to Hurst, he advised me that in 1974 he had authored a book which gave an overview and summary of the main points of the course. He very graciously offered me the rights to reprint that material, and this resulted in the book you are now reading. This completed the project I had in mind from the beginning, to make all of the Hurst research and work available again to the investment community.

The course itself is quite lengthy and will prove exceedingly valuable to those willing to devote the necessary time and effort to studying and mastering the principles of trading it teaches. A longtime Traders Press customer, who manages in excess of $100 million, advised me that the sole method he used in his timing and selection decisions was the Hurst approach as taught in his course. Any reader of this book who is interested in the full course (which is available exclusively through Traders Press) is encouraged to contact Traders Press for full descriptive information. The price paid for this book may be deducted from the price of the course.

It is my hope that my efforts to preserve the work of Hurst will prove helpful to investors who avail themselves of his genius by studying his work.

Sincerely,

Edward D. Dobson

Edward D. Dobson, President
Traders Press, Inc.
Greenville, SC
October 12, 1999

About the Author

James M. Hurst was educated at Kansas State, Brown, and Washington Universities, majoring in physics and mathematics. World War II and the advent of radar stimulated interest and training in electronics and the theory of communications.

Following the war, Mr. Hurst specialized for 25 years in electronics systems design for aerospace applications. An interesting project related to antisubmarine warfare provided experience with and appreciation of the power of large digital computers as applied to the problem of extracting information from time-series data.

Numerical analysis methods were first applied by Mr. Hurst to negotiable equity data in the search for a solution to the classical cost-effectiveness problem. This effort led to the discovery of the spectral signature phenomenon in price data (cyclicality), and to a *Theory of Irrational Decision Processes*. *The Wave Theory of Price Action* described in this paper is the first practical application of *The Decision Theory* to be developed.

In 1969, Mr. Hurst founded **Decision Models, Inc.** for the purpose of further developing decision theory and wave concepts as applied to the equity markets. The **CycliTec** aids to cyclic analysis of equities resulted and were initially published in 1971.

Mr. Hurst has authored several treatises on the Wave Theory of Price Action. The first was the book *The Profit Magic of Stock Transaction Timing*, published by **Prentice-Hall** in 1970. The paper *Cycles for Profits in Stocks and Commodities* was presented to the Society for the Investigation of Recurring Events on 15 June 1971. The paper *Predictive Implications of Periodicity in Stock and Commodity Prices* followed (presented to the Technical Security Analysts of San Francisco, 18 October 1972). The last, and by far most extensive treatment is in the form of the *CycliTec Services Training Course*, initially published in 1973 by **CycliTec Services**, San Francisco.

This course has been reproduced and preserved by Traders Press, Inc., Greenville, SC and has been renamed the JM Hurst Cycles Trading and Training Course. It is exclusively available through Traders Press.

Synopsis

The advent of accurate and continuous equity price histories made possible the study of equity price movement as a function of time, independent of all other variables.

Early studies of such data produced the conclusion that equity prices vary in a random, hence unpredictable, way.

This conclusion has been replaced in the last decade as evidence mounts that equity price variation is ordered and quasi-predictable.

The relationship between past and future prices is found to be complex and nonlinear. Current simplified models represent price movement as consisting of a linear combination of wave functions with specific and consistent interrelationships. This viewpoint has led to the development of the Wave Theory of Price Action.

From this Wave Theory, a body of practical applications methods called *Cyclic Analysis* has been evolved which permits a fully integrated and wholly technical approach to the problem of trading and investing successfully in the stock and commodity markets.

This approach features the following unique capabilities: prediction of price-reversal timing, prediction of the price at an anticipated reversal, estimation of the extent of the price move expected to follow a reversal, and evaluation of a transaction before entry in terms of risk and profit potential.

Cyclic Analysis methodology has been field tested since 1971, and computerized analysis aids are available.

$\mathcal{P}$reface

Until 1979 my career followed the established path of university scientists and teachers the world over—writing papers, teaching students, presenting my work at conferences and visiting other workers in my field of scientific research. Then I was invited to spend a year as visiting scientist with the Food and Drug Administration in Washington, D. C., bringing my family with me.

Since I had an interest in the stock market, mainly from the scientific aspect of using digital filters to market data, I naturally paid a visit to the local library to see what was available on the subject of investment. I was astonished to find almost a whole wall of books devoted to this topic, at a time when there would have been probably none, or at best a couple of books on this subject back home in our local library in England.

Imagine my delight and pleasure when after about three months I came across J. M. Hurst's book *The Profit Magic of Stock Transaction Timing* (published by Prentice Hall). Unknown to me, Hurst had been putting into practice for years methods of analysis of market data that I had only recently begun to look at. Hurst was a mathematical analyst with an engineering background and he employed techniques familiar to me as a scientist where I frequently analyzed the noisy output of various instruments. He also, in his book, satisfied the slight reservations I had as a scientist about the predictability of the stock market by providing a great deal of evidence in support of the author's theories about cycles and channels in stock price movement.

If I had any criticism of the book at all, it was simply that the average investor, picking it up and quickly scanning through its pages, would perhaps feel that it was too mathematically orientated, and replace it on the shelf, because it contained terms such as *Fourier Analysis, modulated sidebands,* etc. The investor would then be missing an important contribution to the subject of technical analysis. However, a reader who took the trouble to study the book in depth would grasp that Hurst's work was based on five main concepts. These were:

1. Maximum profits are obtained from shorter trades
2. Some 23% of price motion is based on cyclic movements in nature
3. These cycles are additive

4.   The cycles can be seen clearly if envelopes are constructed around the price movement
5.   The ideal buying point is when several such cyclic components are reaching their low points

Now, some 20 years later, Hurst's pioneering work is as valid as ever, and his concepts form a solid foundation for profitable investment. To my regret, I never had the opportunity of meeting Hurst, but I can truly say that he was responsible for changing my life, because once I returned to England I used his basic principles as a starting point for my own line of research into price movements. This soon became my full time occupation.

Of course, I have the advantage over Hurst of state-of the-art computers and vast amounts of price data from markets all around the world on stocks, commodities, currencies and futures. However, these markets all have one thing in common—the methods described in this book apply to all of them, as will be seen by the examples used to illustrate the various chapters.

In this book I have employed the general principle of putting forward a concept and then applying it to artificial data before using it on real market data. The reason for this is quite simple—predictive techniques must be shown to work with totally predictable data, i.e. artificial data, so that the accuracy of the predictions can be checked. It is only then that these same techniques can be applied to less predictable market data.

A great deal of space has also been taken by a full discussion of moving averages and their properties. Moving averages are not only simple to calculate, they are also extremely powerful tools, but unfortunately the majority of investors have no idea of how to harness this power. It is to be hoped that the treatment given here will enable readers to avoid the mistakes made by using them incorrectly.

Finally, although the majority of investors have access to computers and programs to carry out various calculations and plot charts, computers are not absolutely essential for channel analysis, and the investor with only a pencil, paper and calculator can still achieve a great improvement in performance.

—Brian J. Millard, Bramhall Cheshire England

Introduction

The corporation concept has been in existence since the thirteen hundreds—and negotiable equities on the North American Continent date from the issuance of **Hudson Bay Company** stock in about 1670.

Despite this long history, it wasn't until after the turn of the last century that serious thought was given to why equity prices vary, and in what manner. At about that time several important events took place:

1.   1889. *The Wall Street Journal* came into existence, and with it, a wealth of accurate and readily available information on price movements as a function of time.

2.   1896. The Dow Jones Averages were created and published. This provided graphic visibility to the form of price change versus time.

3.   1900. *Louis Bachelier* wrote his provocative and scholarly paper *"Theory of Speculation"* that became the basis for the random-walk theory of price variation. (1)

4.   1902. *S. A. Nelson* compiled **Charles Dow's** ideas in *The ABC of Stock Speculation.* (2)

Thus, within this brief span of time, documented price data became available, the random-walk theory was proposed, and one of the first technical approaches to stock market trading and investment was born.

In the following years, market enthusiasts split into three distinct groups:

1. *Fundamentalists*, holding that price movements principally reflect changes in the circumstances related to a company and its products or activities

2. *Academicians*, unable to improve significantly on the Bachelier premise that price Movements are random within reflecting bounds

3. *Technicians*, finding particular, frequently recurring, price patterns in the past to be the harbingers of prices to come.

None of these three viewpoints really comes to grips with the problem of making money consistently in the stock and commodity markets.

The random-walk theory discourages all hope of capitalizing on price fluctuations.

Fundamentalists must similarly ignore the immense profit potential of price oscillations. Furthermore, the occurrence of fundamental forcing functions is found to be nearly as unpredictable as price change is held to be by the random-walk theory.

Classical technical analysis has demonstrated serious deficiencies. While the frequent appearance of empirically defined price patterns is a definite fact, applications have suffered from lack of a coherent theory on which to base methodology.

Furthermore, none of the existing approaches provides a basis for a self-contained, logical, and complete solution to the money-management problems of issue selection, transaction timing, and transaction yield optimization.

Fortunately, recent years have seen the birth of a fourth viewpoint in which such capabilities are inherent. This viewpoint is based on the *Wave Theory of Price Action*, and the landmarks of development are indicated by the following events:

1. 1938. **Ralph Nelson Elliott** published his well-known monograph *"The Wave Principle."* (3)

2.   1940. In Pittsburgh, The Foundation for the Study of Cycles was formed.

3.   1958. The Society for the Investigation of Recurring Events was organized in New York.

4.   1960. The author initiated a study of the way in which human decisions are made.

Equity price data was chosen for this study on the assumption that price changes reflect human decision processes. Unexpected results were obtained in the course of computerized spectral analyses of this data. It was found that price movement can be described as a complex combination of periodic functions with specific interrelationships. This work has continued to the present, resulting in a *Theory of Irrational Decision Processes*.

5.   1971. An outgrowth of the Theory of Irrational Decision Processes was the Wave Theory of Price Action. A book was published by the author describing practical applications of Wave Theory to the timing of stock market transactions. (4)

6.   1971. Computerized aids to Wave Theory analysis of stock and commodity price histories became available for public use. (5)

7.   1973. The first complete description of wave concepts as applied to the capital management problem was published. (6)

The common element between these and other related events was the mounting evidence Independently offered by hundreds of researchers that a remarkable degree of periodicity characterizes time-series data describing a wide range of real-world situations – among these, the price movement of auction-market equities.

In the last decade several facts have emerged as outstanding:

1.   There is very little of the random in the price movement of negotiable equities.

2. Fundamental considerations do enter the picture, but in a quite unexpected way.

3. The price movement of negotiable equities consists almost entirely of a complex combination of wave motions with many of the predictive implications of simple wave functions.

4. The same wave functions and characteristics discovered in equity prices are found to be operative in many other situations as well.

Thus, seventy years after the events that first made it possible to question whether or not a governing law exists behind the apparently aimless meandering of equity prices, some of the answers are beginning to emerge. And these answers have exciting implications.

The reason why fundamental studies fail to predict price oscillations is now known, as well as the manner in which fundamentals actually do enter the picture.

The reasons behind the empirically developed axioms of classical charting methods are now apparent, as well as the causes for frequent failure of these methods in application.

The reason for the erroneous conclusion on the part of Bachelier (and others) that equity price movement is essentially random is now understood.

Even more important, the art that has been called *technical analysis* has now become far less an art and much more a science. Methods of making use of the predictive capability implicit in the developing *Wave Theory of Price Action* are presently in existence and in use—and prediction of future equity price movement, however imperfect, is the name-of-the-game in trading and investing.

The remainder of this article will describe in brief the methods now being employed for making use of the *Wave Theory of Price Action*.

An Evolving Natural Law

In the last ten years it has become increasingly evident that the wide-spread periodicity observed in many kinds of data implies a common cause, or forcing function. Such universal and common forcing functions are usually ascribed to a law of nature. In this instance, the emerging natural law can be stated as follows:

> *Numerous real-world situations, including the price behavior of negotiable equities, reflect a common, complex, periodic forcing function. Change in the affected situations is describable as the sum of many simple wave functions. The particular waves composing the sum are a specific, describable subset in the infinity of possible such subsets. The relationships between wave variables are reasonably constant and are common to all of the situations involved.*

The commonality feature implied in this law is remarkable and quite general. The same wave functions and wave-variable relationships are found to be operating in the price movement of all stocks, commodities, bonds warrants, rights, etc.—whether traded on the New York, Tokyo, London, or other exchanges, and without regard for the time period considered.

Even more remarkable, all or a portion of the same specific wave subset is dominant in the time variations of weather data, grasshopper abundance, tree ring formations, lynx procreation, bacteria division rates, and the catch of fisheries, to name only a few of the reported examples.

This natural law, as applied to explain the price movement of negotiable equities, is the *Wave Theory of Price Action* mentioned in the preceding section. Methodology developed to apply his theory to trading and investment problems is called *Cyclic Analysis*.

WAVE FUNCTIONS AND
RELATIONSHIPS IN PRICE MOVEMENT

The Wave Theory of Price Action is embodied in a set of eight Basic Principles of Cyclicality as described in reference 6. The most significant relationships involved have to do with *waves*, the elemental building blocks of periodic processes.

An ideal wave (shown in figure 1) varies smoothly and uniformly about a value of zero, alternately assuming positive and negative values. One complete repetition of a wave is called a *cycle*.

Only three parameters are required to completely characterize a wave (see figure 1):

1.   *Period*, the length of time elapsed from trough to trough

2.   *Amplitude*, the size of the wave from trough to crest

3.   *Phase*, the time position of the wave with respect to any given reference time.

In figure 1 the phase parameter has been transformed to the more useful quantity *phase difference*, which is a measure of the relative position in time of one wave with respect to another.

The most important wave characteristic is periodicity. As one cycle of a wave is completed, another identical cycle is commenced. It is readily apparent that once the three basic parameters of a wave are known, the value of the wave can then be ascertained for all possible values of time— *including the future*. It is this ingredient of the *Wave Theory of Price Action* that implies predictability of future price movement.

The Principles of Cyclicality state that the price movements of all negotiable equities consist of the sum of the same set of waves with the same interconnecting relationships between the wave variables (period, amplitude, and phase). Thus, price history differences among equities are due solely to minor variations in the values of these wave variables at any given time, with the minor variations in wave variables causing large variations in the sum due to the large number of waves involved.

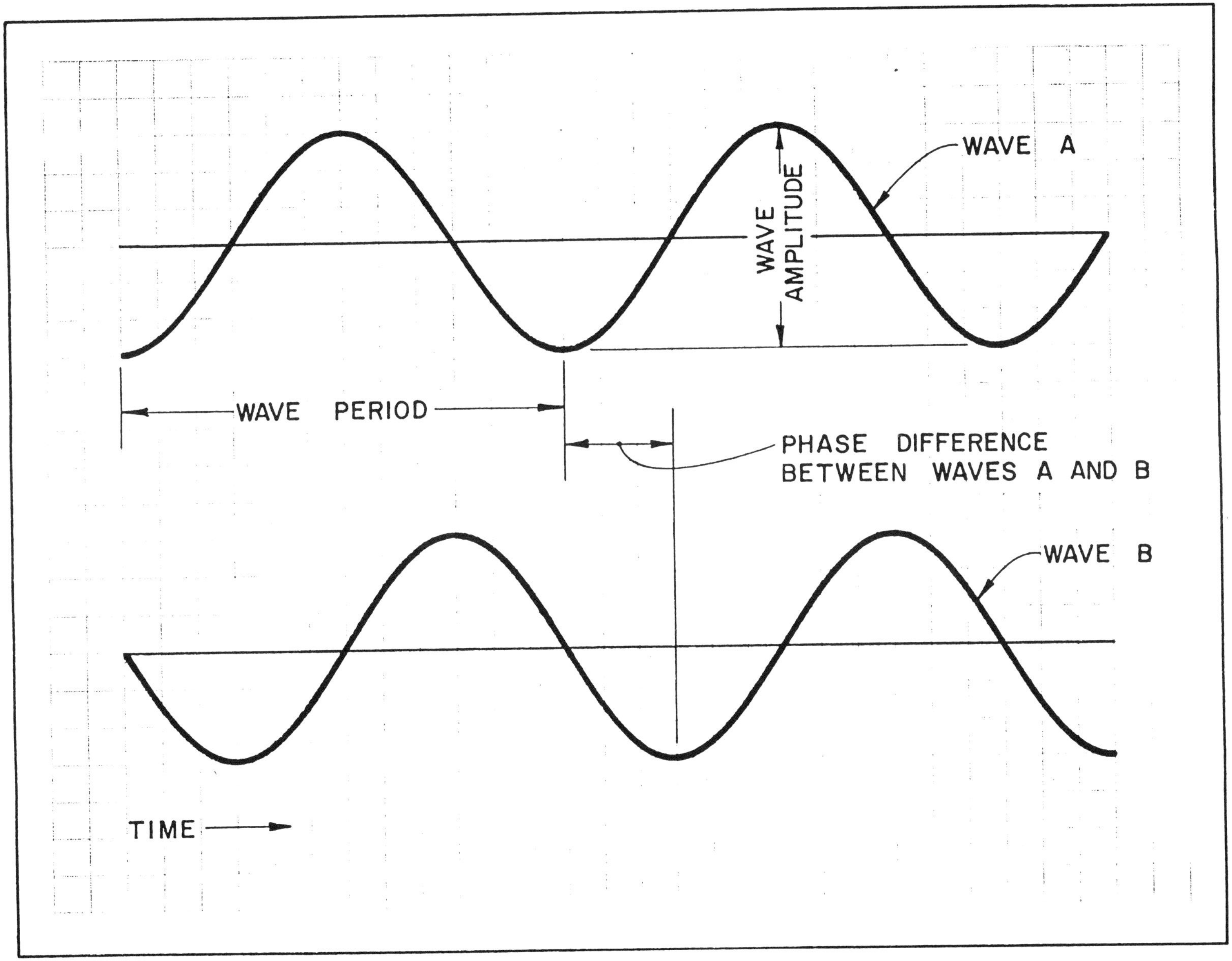

Figure 1 - Basic Price Waves

There is no known limit to the number of waves in the set that combine to form equity price movement. Some of these waves have periods measured in minutes, while others require many years to complete one cycle.

Fortunately, it is not necessary to identify and sum all such waves in order to make use of the phenomena. Only a rather small number of waves is needed to permit useful conclusions to be drawn regarding the probable future course of equity prices.

Thus, the potentially vast complexities of the Wave Theory of Price Action are reduced to the relatively simple effects and characteristics of a finite set of waves. The resulting simplified model is then used as the basis for Cyclic Analysis.

Price waves exhibit a series of extremely significant interrelationships that are identified in the Principles of Cyclicality. The most important of these are as follows:

1. The periods of the component waves vary about, but remain close to, a particular subset in the infinity of possible subsets of periods. This relationship is referred to **nominality**.

2. The ratio of the average periods of contiguous waves in the nominal wave set is a small, whole number, usually two. This is known as the property of **harmonicity**.

3. The amplitudes of waves in the nominal set are approximately in proportion to the wave periods. This is the property of **proportionality**.

4. The waves in the set are so phased as to cause wave troughs to occur Simultaneously whenever consistent with harmonicity. This property is referred to as **synchronicity**.

5. Total price action consists of the algebraic sum of all waves operating in a given equity at a given time. This is a statement of the linear wave combination property and is spoken of as the *summation* effect.

6. An additional relationship, known as the property of **variation**, will be dealt with in the next section.

These not-to-be-expected, but highly useful, wave relationships are responsible for most of the characteristics of equity price movement—including the recurring pattern phenomena of most classical charting methods. The implications are enormous, and the whole of Cyclic Analysis is founded on these premises.

The nominal wave periods referred to in relationship 1 are further simplified for ease of remembering to a nearly harmonic set as follows:

WAVE PERIODS

Years	Months	Weeks	Days
18			
9			
	54		
	18		
		40	
		20	
			80
			40
			20
			10
			5

This set of wave periods is spoken of as the ***nominal cyclic model***. It should be noted that an important exception to the period ratio of two occurs in the case of the 18- and 54-month waves, the periods of which are related by a factor of three.

The property of proportionality implies that the amplitude of the nominal 10-day wave is twice that of the 5-day wave, etc.— but that the amplitude of the 54-month wave is three times that of the 18-month wave.

The properties of synchronicity and harmonicity lead to the expectation that at the time of a trough of any given name, a trough will also occur for each wave of shorter period. Thus, wave troughs tend to form in groups called ***nests-of-lows***. The converse is true at wave crests in that synchronicity and harmonicity preclude time groupings of wave crests. This effect is responsible for the narrow, sharp bottoms and the rounded, oscillatory tops that characterize equity price movement.

The phenomenon is illustrated in figure 2, where a set of three ideal, synchronous, harmonic, proportional waves are summed to produce a simple composite wave representative of price movement. The diamonds below the composite wave show the time locations of the troughs of waves A, B, and C and the resultant nexts-of-lows. The triangles above the composite wave are located at the time positions of the crests of waves A, B, and C and show how wave crests fail to occur in groups. The composite wave itself shows the characteristic sharp bottoms and rounded, oscillatory top found in actual price movement.

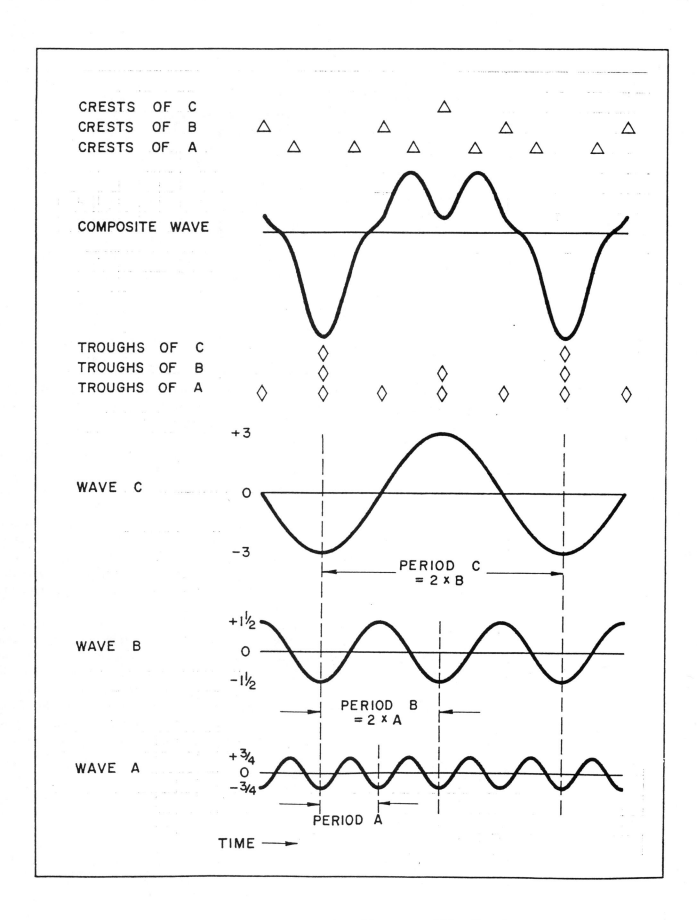

Figure 2 - Effects of Harmonic Periods and Synchronized Wave Troughs

THE INTERACTION BETWEEN
WAVES AND FUNDAMENTAL EVENTS

The description given so far of price motion as a function of waves is ultra simplistic. The complexities encountered in assembling a useful model of price change can, however, be conveniently grouped under the heading of *wave modulation*.

When three or more ideal waves having certain specified interrelationships are summed (the periods are not harmonically related, but are rather close together), a special modification of a single ideal wave is produced. Such a modified wave is said to be *modulated*. A modulated wave retains most of the predictive advantages of an ideal wave, but amplitude and period fluctuate slowly as time passes.

In actual price movement, it is found that the waves in the nominal cyclic model are not single ideal waves at all. Instead, each wave is made up of a bundle of closely spaced waves that sum to form a modulated wave. The average periods of these modulated waves correspond with those given in the nominal cyclic model.

The fluctuations in the period and amplitude of these modulated waves are referred to as the property of *variation*.

This property of price waves is then further complicated by the effect of fundamental events. The impact of news releases, earnings expectations, product development, and the like is wholly absorbed as an orderly amplitude change in a contiguous-period subset of the nominal cyclic model. The result is additional modulation of the basic price waves.

The extent of fundamentally induced amplitude variation and the number of waves affected depends on the nature of the fundamental event and on the degree to which this event alters volume interest in the equity.

The all-important result of this behavior is that fundamental events do not disturb the periods or phases of price waves— and therefore do not disturb price movement timing predictions. Instead, the wave amplitude changes involved cause a change in price volatility. If a fundamental event has a high impact or is persistent, waves with relatively long periods will undergo amplitude changes. When this happens, the equity price will exhibit a relatively long lasting rise or fall (depending on the nature of the fundamental event) upon which the oscillations of the shorter waves are superimposed. These fairly common long lasting rises or falls are termed *pseudo trends* and may persist for weeks, months, or even years. They are produced entirely by the normal summing of waves in the cyclic model, but the longer waves in the model have undergone amplitude changes as a result of a fundamental event.

From a theoretical standpoint, the interaction of fundamentals with cyclicality can be considered to be a part of the modulation effect already present.

In the light of this curious behavior of price waves in response to fundamental events, several previously puzzling aspects of price movement can be explained:

1. Cyclic predictions, such as the price reversals at nests-of-lows, are made entirely on the basis of past price history. Yet, invariably, when these predictions come to pass, a suitable fundamental event is present to "account" for the resulting price response.

    If the subsequent price movement is in accordance with the usual expectations for a cyclic model with normal wave amplitudes, then it is likely that the fundamental event cited as "causing" the price reversal was merely the one event, among the many events that are always available, that was selected by the analyst as best fitting the circumstances under consideration.

    If the subsequent price movement exhibits a pseudo trend, either short-term or long-term, then it is likely that a true fundamental interaction is present. Further, it is likely that the fundamental event was in synchronism with the cyclic model for equity price movement because it was brought about by the same human decision processes that produce price movement.

2. The use of Cyclic Analysis by a large number of investors does not destroy the wave behavior of price movement.

    Such use constitutes an alteration in volume interest, which is the intermediate result of any fundamental event. Thus, the effect on price waves is identical to that produced by any other fundamental event; namely, amplitude increase in a subset of waves resulting in volatility change, but no change in price-reversal timing.

3. Fundamental events such as the activities of Federal agencies in regulating money supply can be shown to correlate with price behavior around 54-month price lows and highs. Yet such 54-month waves have been present in price movement throughout market history, including the time before these agencies existed.

This observation is subject to the same explanatory comment as item 1 and serves to emphasize the point.

It is this very important relationship between fundamental events and price wave amplitudes that makes possible a wholly technical basis for forming stock and commodity transaction decisions.

THE QUANTIFICATION OF TRENDS USING WAVE CONCEPTS

One of the most immediate results of the *Wave Theory of Price Action* is the clarification of what is meant by *trend*. This clarification leads directly to operations of great importance in Cyclic Analysis.

The ideas involved are best illustrated by use of a graphic display of wave parameters known as a ***Periodogram***. Figure 3 depicts a Periodogram for a portion of the nominal cyclic model.

In a Periodogram, wave amplitude is plotted as a function of wave period. Each vertical line of figure 3 is, therefore, an indication of the existence of one of the waves of the nominal cyclic model. A study of this figure will show that the idealized characteristics of nominality, harmonicity, and proportionality have been incorporated.

Now the property of summation is drawn upon. Suppose that we break down the set of waves that we have called the nominal cyclic model into two mutually exclusive subsets and that we sum each of these two subsets. By the Associative Law of Addition, the total price movement that is the sum of the waves in the nominal cyclic model can be equally well represented by the sum of the two subset sums.

Let us choose for these two subset sums:

1.   The sum of all waves of period equal to, and shorter than, any one arbitrarily selected wave

2.   The sum of all waves of period longer than the arbitrarily selected wave.

This set division is indicated in figure 3 by the vertical line A (as one of the possible choices).

It follows that the composite wave composed of the longer period waves is a smoother function than the composite wave composed of the shorter period waves. Furthermore,

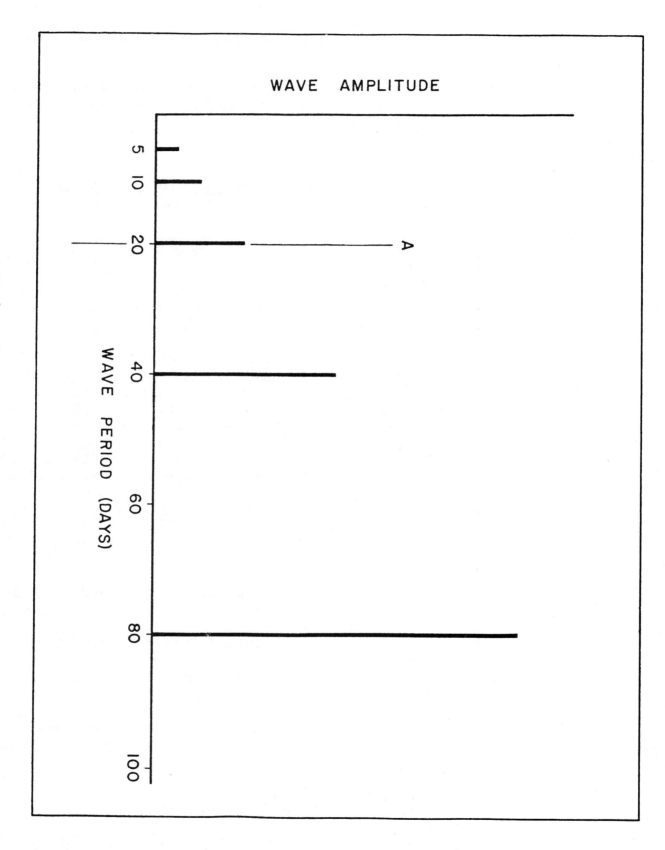

Figure 3 - A Periodogram Representation of a Portion of the Nominal Cyclic Model

the latter composite wave, when summed with the former and then overlaid on it for display, must appear to oscillate regularly above and below the smoother function.

This smooth function composed of the longer period waves is now defined to be the trend underlying the composite wave composed of the shorter period waves.

From this definition it is apparent that:

1.   A trend can be established for any desired price wave of a cyclic mode.

2.   There are as many trends operative in price movement as there are price waves.

3.   Some trends can be up at the same time that others are down.

4.   If component wave amplitudes, periods, and phases are known, any selected trend can be evaluated in the form of a price rate for any desired time —including the future.

It is difficult to overstate the practical importance of this definitization of the otherwise nebulous idea of trend.

Not only is the opportunity presented for the quantitative prediction of a given trend in the form of a price rate, but a similar evaluation can be made simultaneously for all possible trends. From among these, the trend that is most suitable to support predetermined investment yield objectives can then be selected.

Also, meaningful interpretations are now possible for the graphic constructions known as *trendlines*. Such lines, drawn by rules derived from Wave Theory, now signal the occurrence of wave events—and can be used intelligently as action signals. These kinds of trendlines are renamed *valid trendlines*, or *VTL's*, to avoid confusion with the less specific traditional trendlines.

VTL's can also be employed as graphic tools to aid in the isolation and identification of component waves from raw price data.

The rules for constructions of VTL's and the methods of usage are detailed in reference 6.

PREDICTING PRICE REVERSAL TIMING

The trend and trading cycle definitions that are derived from Wave Theory are significant benefits of great practical utility. Nevertheless, these accomplishments of the wave viewpoint are minor by comparison with the following two logical extensions:

1.   Ability to estimate price reversal timing *in the future*

2.   Ability to estimate the extent of the price moves that will occur *both prior and subsequent to anticipated price reversals.*

These two capabilities provide the potential for a fully-integrated approach to trading and investing.

The first capability will be discussed in this section, and the second in the section to follow.

It is clear that practical use of wave concepts is dependent on the ability to separate individual wave components from past price data and to estimate the periods and phases of these waves. The Cyclic Analysis process used to accomplish these aims is called *formal phasing analysis*, or *FPA*. The methods employed in conducting an FPA are predominantly graphical and include the use of computer generated aids. (5) These methods are described in detail in reference 6.

An FPA results in the identification of the time position of each trough of each wave of the cyclic model active in a given issue at the time of the analysis. From this information the average period and the phase of each wave are obtained.

The average wave period and the period variation experienced in the past are then extrapolated from the latest identified wave trough, repeatedly, until the trough timing for each wave of interest is estimated for any desired portion of future time. In this way, estimated time positions (with tolerance limits) for future nests-of-lows are established.

Powerful assistance in the process of wave trough location is provided by the properties of nominality, harmonicity, and synchronicity through the following considerations:

1.   The resulting wave period estimates must fall within a known range of the nominal Wave periods.

2.   The known harmonic relationships between contiguous wave periods must not be violated.

3.   The estimated future time positions of successive wave troughs must continue the synchronized pattern of trough locations established in past time.

Price reversals in the upward direction are then expected to take place at the estimated times established for future nests-of-lows—within the tolerance range determined in the FPA. The number of wave troughs involved in a nest-of-lows provides an immediate indication of the potential strength of the reversal.

Price reversals in the downward direction are predicted by establishing the estimated time positions of future wave crests. Since these crests are not synchronized, the actual component wave whose crest is most likely to be associated with the price high is determined from predictions of future trend and the resulting time translation of price high relative to wave crest.

From the foregoing, it can be seen that Wave Theory provides a way to estimate in a logical fashion the future time of occurrence of price reversals that will be followed by price moves of any desired magnitude in either direction.

The Cyclic Analysis methodology used in the prediction of price-reversal timing is demonstrated in figure 5. This is a typical graphic display of the kind in use for the analysis of stocks and commodities. (5) The price and time gridlines normally present have been removed for the sake of clarity in reproduction.

An FPA has been performed and the wave trough locations are indicated by diamonds below the price bars. The Periodogram at the bottom of the chart is computer-generated and provides estimates of the wave components active in this particular equity at the time of the analysis. This Periodogram and the smooth envelope enclosing the price bars are the primary computer-generated tools used in carrying out the FPA.

The average wave periods resulting from the FPA are shown to the far right of the associated rows of diamonds, and several of the extrapolated future time positions of nests-of-lows are indicated. The expectation demonstrated is for a price reversal in the upward direction to occur in approximately two to three weeks, powered by the reversal of all waves up to and including the nominal 18-month wave.

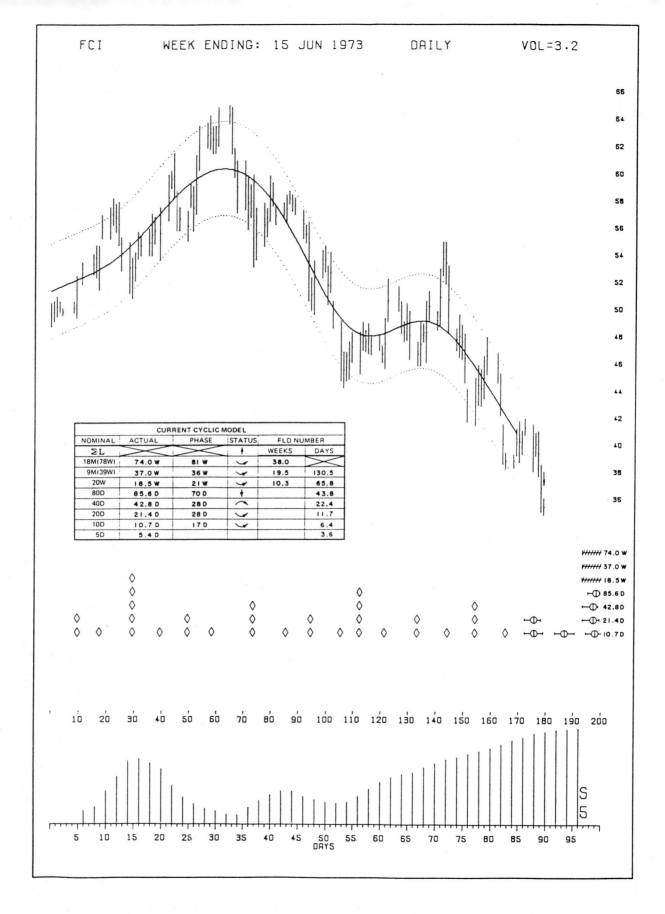

Figure 4 - A Typical Forming Phasing Analysis

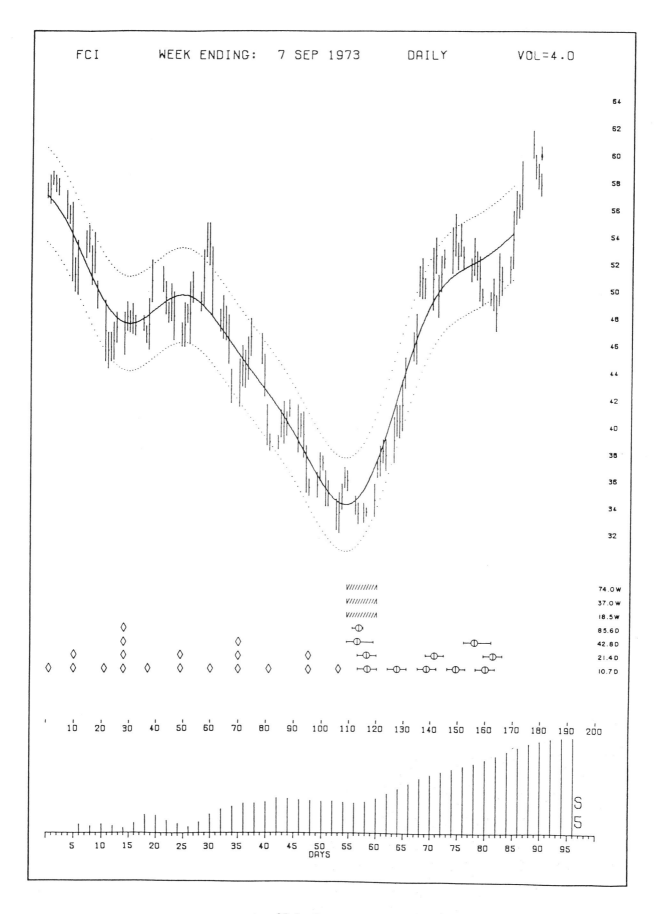

Figure 5 -   Results of Price Reversal Timing Prediction

The tabulation shown on the chart is known as a *current cyclic model* and is a compact way of organizing the information gained from an FPA. In this table, the periods of the nominal cyclic model are shown to the left for comparison with the actual FPA average periods obtained. Wave phase is tabulated in terms of time elapsed since the last identified wave trough. The arrows shown are developed from phase status and show the current direction of action of each wave. The columns at the far right contain numbers derived from average wave periods which permit construction of the graphic devices to price-move prediction that will be described in the next section.

Figure 6 shows the same equity at a later time with the price-reversal timing predictions from Figure 5 overlaid for comparison. It is seen that the predicted timing was very close indeed and that the reversal resulted in a price move from 32 to the 60's. Except for predictable minor oscillations, prices subsequently moved uninterruptedly to the region of 90 before the effects of this powerful nest-of-lows subsided.

PREDICTING THE EXTENT OF PRICE MOVES

Foretelling when a price reversal is likely to occur is a powerful capability, but the ability to similarly estimate how far prices are most likely to move following a reversal *even before such a reversal takes place* is, without question, the crowning achievement of Wave Theory.

This potential is provided by a graphical construction, unique to the wave viewpoint, called the *future line of demarcation, or FLD*.

An FLD is a theoretical barrier, constructed in future chart time, dividing price-time space into two parts. The interaction, at some later time, of actual prices with this barrier is used to answer critical wave questions. The wave question of primary interest in price prediction is: "How much farther is a given wave and its associated trend likely to drive prices before that wave forms its next trough or crest?"

Figure 7 demonstrates how an FLD works for the case of a single, ideal price wave.

In Figure 7a, a price wave is shown up to the time A. The dashed wave section market *FLD* is a replica of the price wave, but displaced to the right (into future time) by one-half of the period of the price wave.

In Figure 7b, the same situation is shown except that time has progressed to D and the FLD has been extended in to the future by a corresponding amount. Notice that the price wave has interacted with its FLD at C.

Figure 7 demonstrates that an FLD is possessed of the following characteristics:

1.   In future time, the FLD associated with a given wave is rising where the wave will be falling when that time is reached.

2.   In future time, the FLD associated with a given wave forms a trough where the wave will form a crest when that time is reached. (See time B in Figure 7.) Similarly, the FLD forms a crest where the wave will form a trough when that time is reached.

3.   When a wave intersects its FLD, that wave is *one-half way along on its move down or up*, depending on whether the crossing is down or up, respectively. (See Time C in Figure 7.)

While the first two properties are very useful, in effect, painting a picture in future time of wave action to be, it is the third FLD characteristic that provides the potential for prediction of price-move magnitude.

Although figure 7 illustrates the FLD concept, actual price movement is far more complex than the simple wave of this figure, and the operation of an FLD for these more complex wave forms is much more difficult to visualize.

Let us assume that the component waves active in a given equity at a given time have been isolated by the FPA process so that estimates of wave period and phase are available. An FLD associated with any given wave is then constructed by displacing past price data forward in time by one-half of the estimated period of the selected wave. Such an FLD can be constructed for each wave of a current cyclic model.

The ideal operation of an FLD is distorted by the fact that the displaced price data consists of a complex sum of waves rather than a simple single wave. Nevertheless, the wave properties of harmonicity and proportionality combine in price movement in such a manner as to permit extremely useful conclusions to be drawn from the interrelationships of prices and FLD's.

For example, when prices are below an FLD and rising, the price at intersection with the FLD is theoretically half along on the way up from the price low at the last trough of the wave on which the FLD is based. Similarly, when prices are above an FLD and falling, the price at intersection is theoretically halfway along on the way down from the price high at the last crest of the wave on which the FLD is based.

In practice, such FLD price move projections are refined by evaluation of trend underlying the wave on which the FLD is based. FLD projections are then expected to be undershot when underlying trend opposes the anticipated move, met when trend is flat, and overshot when trend supports the anticipated move.

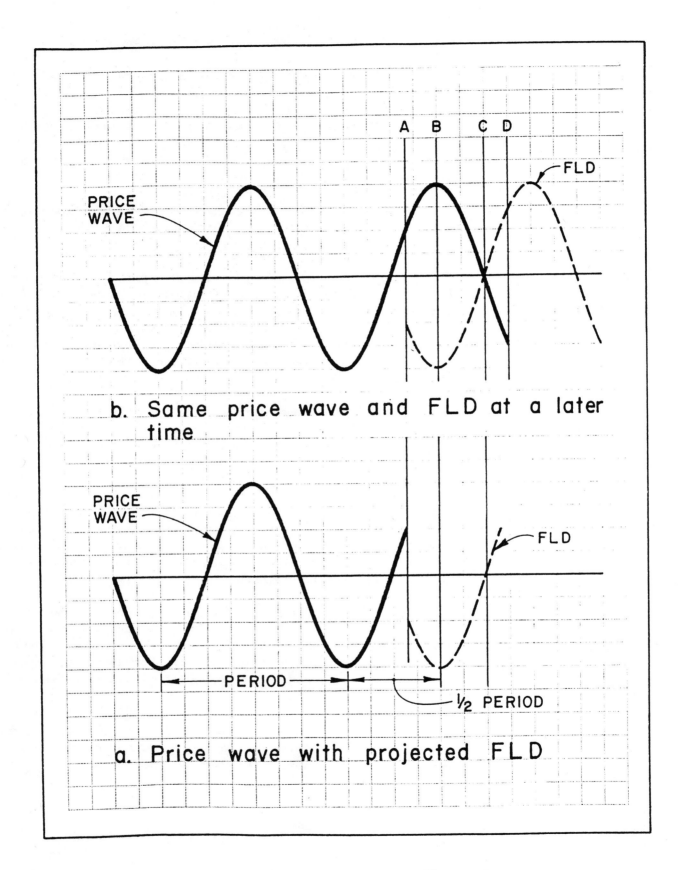

Figure 6 - The Future Line of Demarcation

In the case of a downward price objective, the property of synchronicity makes possible a further refinement in the accuracy of the projection. By constructing two FLD's based on two different component waves, the analyst is able to find two different FLD projections applying to the same price move, one of which is to be undershot and the other overshot. The future price move is then expected to terminate in the price range bounded by the two FLD projections. This price range, when combined with the price-reversal time range predicted from an FPA, results in a price-time box for a future price move.

The FLD is an extremely versatile tool and is used in numerous ways in Cyclic Analysis. For example, FLD's can be constructed equally well in past time. By observing the degree to which actual price movement fulfilled past-time FLD predictions, the trend underlying any given wave can be further quantified. This information can then be used to refine future-time FLD projections.

Past-time FLD's are also invaluable in the FPA process of isolating and identifying component wave trough time positions.

Further, because of the precise nature of FLD's and their tight relationships to wave events, FLD's become near ideal future-time action signal generators.

But the real power of the FLD resides in the meaning of the patterns formed by FLD sets. One particularly useful pattern is discussed in the next section.

Figures 8 and 9 show an example of the use of a single FLD in the prediction of the magnitude of a future price move.

In this instance, an FPA provided a period estimate of 73.6 weeks as the current-time equivalent of the nominal 18-month wave active in the Dow Jones Industrial Average (DJIA). In figure 8, the FLD associated with this wave is shown, and prices are seen rising from the last 73.6-week wave trough to an intersection with the FLD in mid-February of 1972. At that time the FLD intersection created a price projection to 1044 (the price move from the last 73.6-week price low to the FLD break added to the price at the FLD break). The following eleven weeks are also shown, with prices making progress toward the objective.

In figure 9, subsequent weeks are shown through 2 February 1973. At the time of this chart, the price high for this nominal 18-month wave had formed, and prices had reached (and slightly exceeded) the objective. Following weeks saw a to-be-expected price decline to the vicinity of 880 as the next 18-month nest-of-lows came about.

In this example, trend underlying the 18-month wave was flat as the objective was approached, and as a consequence the price projection was expected to be approximately met (as it was) rather than overshot or undershot. Thus, more than 10 months in advance, this FLD price projection correctly predicted a price rise in the DJIA from about 920 to over 1040.

Furthermore, not only can long range price objectives such as this be established, but Cyclic Analysis provides the means whereby the extent and timing of all of the intervening price oscillations may be similarly evaluated.

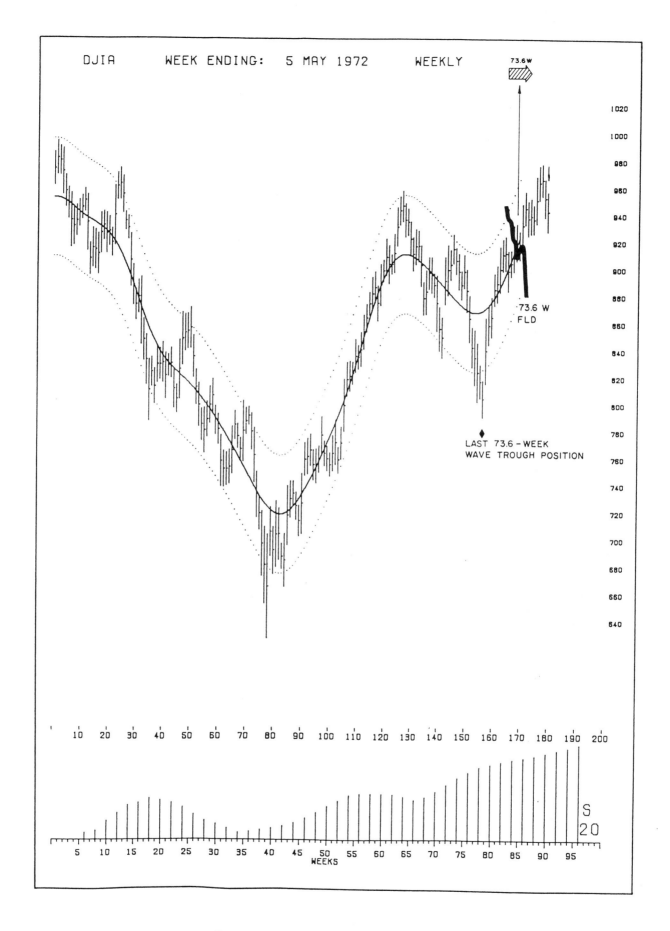

Figure 7 - A Single FLD Price Prediction

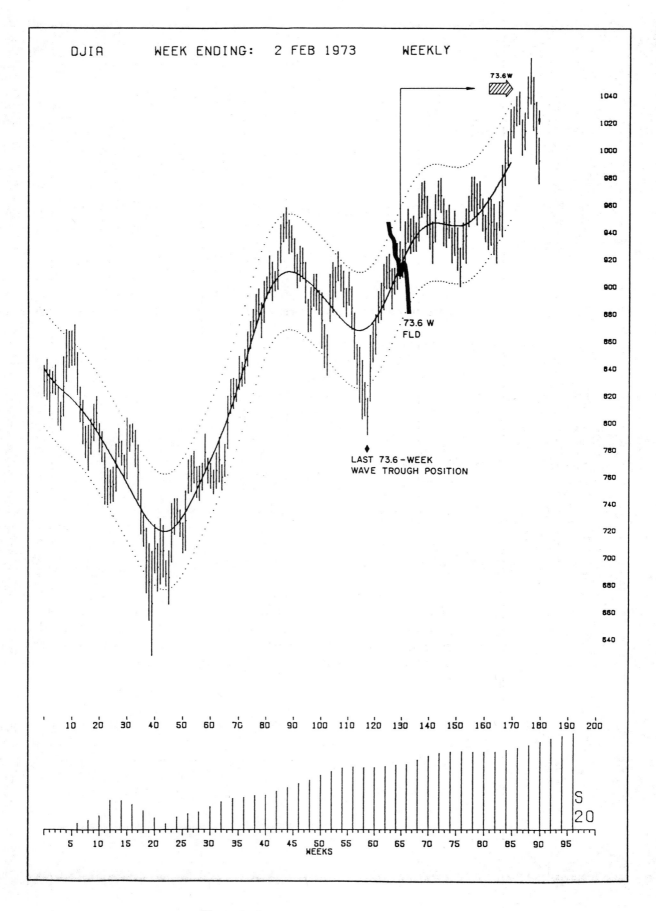

Figure 8 - Results of a Single FLD Price Prediction

THE CASCADE PRINCIPLE

One of the multiple FLD patterns alluded to in the last section is of key importance in the development of a complete trading system. This is the versatile ***FLD cascade pattern.***

Single FLD projections are a significant achievement but have one shortcoming. One-half of the price move projected by a price-FLD interaction is already in the past at the time the projection takes place. The FLD cascade pattern overcomes this deficiency.

At a time when prices are falling, it will be found that some FLD's will be above prices and falling also. The longer prices have been falling, the greater will be the number of FLD's found above prices.

The reverse is true for rising prices: FLD's will be found below prices and rising; and the longer prices have been rising, the greater will be the number of FLD's found below prices.

As a price-reversal point is neared, these FLD's will exhibit spacings such that a price break of an FLD based on a short-period wave will predict a price move that will break a longer-wave FLD. This break will in turn predict a larger price move that will break an FLD based on a still longer wave, etc. Such a set of successive potential FLD breaks predicting a self-propagating series of price moves is called a *cascade*, and the associated FLD's are said to form an *FLD cascade pattern*.

This immeasurably valuable property of multiple FLD's makes possible the prediction of the extent of a postreversal price move *before the reversal takes place*. It is also the property that makes it possible to use price breaks of FLD's based on very short period waves as action signals for purchases or sales based on much longer trading cycles having much larger impacts on price movement.

RISK-LIMIT LOGIC

It is now seen that the **Wave Theory of Price Action** has the inherent potential for the following powerful capabilities: predetermination of transaction yield; prediction of price-reversal timing; and prediction of postreversal price move magnitude.

One final capability is necessary before a completely integrated and self-contained mode of operation is possible in stock and commodity trading. This is the limitation of capital loss in the event of transaction failure.

Wave Theory satisfies this requirement in the following way:

Assume that a potential transaction is foreseen based on an upcoming price reversal. This price reversal will take place at the price low associated with an identified, trend-translated wave crest.

If an FLD or VTL is used to generate an action signal for transaction entry, the probabilities are aligned in favor of wave events responsible for the price reversal having indeed started by the time transaction entry is made. Therefore, probabilities are similarly aligned in favor of price movement *not* doubling back to the price associated with the responsible wave trough or crest before the transaction objective has been met. *A logical stop-loss level is thus established just below the price at the last trading cycle wave trough (for long transactions) or just above the price at the last trading cycle time-translated wave crest (for short transactions).*

With this final link in place, Cyclic Analysis can be used to set up a complete operational system tailored for any desired set of investment or trading goals.

A COMPLETE TRADING SYSTEM

A fully integrated trading system must have the following characteristics and capabilities:

1.   Permit preplanned investment goals

2.   Supply issue selection criteria

3.   Permit pretransaction evaluation and comparison for transaction selection purposes

4.   Provide for automatically triggering transaction entry

5.   Provide for intratransaction analysis for the purpose of optimizing transaction termination.

As these capabilities are discussed individually in the following paragraphs, it will be seen that the preplanning of investment goals is closely tied in with several of the other capabilities of the system.

Issue selection is a particularly simple proposition in the application of Cyclic Analysis. Since the approach is wholly technical, the industry represented, the products supplied, and other fundamental considerations are incidental. The equity is considered only as a set of price-time data against which Cyclic Analysis procedures are to be applied. In practice, a set of several equities is maintained in an analyzed condition. Such a set is called a *stable*. Criteria for stable selection include corporate stability, price volatility, equity fluidity, and sufficient uninterrupted data to permit computerized analysis operations. These elements are judged with investment goals in mind.

Pretransaction evaluation is a direct fallout of the Wave Theory analytical processes discussed in previous sections. To develop this point, the following definitions are needed:

1.   *Transaction risk:* the probability that any single transaction will result in a capital loss instead of a capital gain.

2.   *Risk potential* or *risk:* the amount of capital that may be lost if the transaction fails.

3.   *Profit potential* or *potential:* the amount of capital that will be gained if the transaction succeeds.

4.   *Percentage potential:* potential expressed as a percentage of invested capital.

5.   *Potential-risk ratio* or *PR ratio:* the ratio of potential to risk.

In practice, investment goals are preset in terms of these parameters. For example, transaction risk should be set at .5 or less. The PR ratio should be set at 3.0 or more. And the percentage potential should be set at 20% or more.

To illustrate, let us suppose that Cyclic Analysis has identified an upcoming possible long transaction by the usual means of trading cycle potential evaluation and FPA prediction of price-reversal timing. Assume that an FLD cascade pattern predicts a price move to 31 from an expected transaction entry price of about 19. An FLD price objective for the trading cycle low at the upcoming reversal leads to the expectation that the stop-loss can be set at about 17.

Simple relationships connect these transaction variables as follows:

$$B = \frac{(PR \times SL) + S}{PR + 1}$$

$$\% = \frac{100 \times (S - B)}{B}$$

Where B =   Buy price
PR =   Potential-risk ratio
SL =   Stop-loss price
S   =   Sell Price
% =   Percentage potential

Similar relationships are available for short transactions and for margined and commodity trades.

In the example cited, these relationships would be used to produce the following tabulation:

EVALUATION OF LONG TRANSACTION		
Sell 31	Stop Loss 17	
Buy	PR	%Gross
21.67	2	43.05
20.50	3	51.22
19.80	4	56.57
19.33	5	60.37
19.00	6	63.16
18.75	7	65.33
18.56	8	67.03
18.40	9	68.48
18.27	10	69.68

From this tabulation we can arrive at the following conclusions:

1. A buy at the price of 19 would result in a PR ratio of 6.0 and a percentage potential of 63.16%, both quite acceptable.

2. The maximum acceptable buy price is 20.5 because that price would result in the minimum acceptable PR ratio of 3.0. The resulting percentage potential would be 51.22, also acceptable.

The following points should be noted: this evaluation is produced prior to the price reversal on which the planned transaction is based; this evaluation can be compared with those of other potential transactions in order to select the transaction that is most advantageous; and any desired investment goals can be implemented at will by simply changing the acceptable parameter values. Thus, the ability to conduct transaction selection on a quantitative comparative basis has been achieved —along with the preplanning of investment goals.

VTL's and FLD's provide the action signals needed to prevent errors in wave assumptions from increasing transaction risk to unacceptable levels. Once an action signal is selected, equity price movement is tracked to determine the exact transaction entry time, or preset orders are issued to the broker.

Once a transaction is entered, it is continuously monitored by means of intratransaction Cyclic Analysis. Wave and price events are predicted, and actual events are compared with these predictions to determine the *transaction progress situation*.

There are three transaction progress situations: on track, better than expected, and worse than expected. Each transaction progress situation is associated with definitive modes of transaction termination in such a way as to minimize losses and maximize gains.

If the transaction is classified as either better than expected or worse than expected, then a change in the mode of transaction termination.

It should be realized that the operation of a trading system such as the one described here produces a net yield based on results of a series of transactions. For example, suppose, that average transaction risk for a number of transactions taking place during a year's time is as low as 0.5 —meaning that as many as losses are incurred as gains. Such an operation can still be immensely profitable if the PR ratios average 3.0 or better, since the average gain is then 3 timesd the average loss.

Cyclic Analysis has the potential of achieving transaction risks on the order of 0.2 or 0.3, with correspondingly increased profitability.

Conclusion

The steadily accumulating and increasingly convincing evidence of the cyclic character of many natural and man-made phenomena provides a fascinating field for study and research. One result of such research, the Wave Theory of Price Action, grew out of an investigation of man's decision-making processes. Continuing research may eventually uncover a common causative factor behind this and other similar, but seemingly causatively unrelated, phenomena.

In the area of the practical application of this new cyclic knowledge, there is little question that continuing research will lead to increased understanding of the *Wave Theory of Price Action*. Also, the applications methods and techniques embodied in Cyclic Analysis will undoubtedly be improved, particularly in the area of computer-generated aids.

In the meantime, the present state of the art has proven extremely useful. Cyclic Analysis methods have been in the field since December 1971. The techniques involved are documented in detail in reference 6, and the computerized analysis aids described here are available as reference 5.

Summary

The *Wave Theory of Price Action* refutes the random-walk theory while adequately explaining why earlier studies resulted in the random-walk hypothesis.

In addition, a theoretical basis for technical analysis of stock price movement is established, explaining both the successes and the failures of classical charting methods.

Interactive relationships exist between fundamental factors and wave forcing functions such that the nature of both is preserved.

A body of applications techniques known as Cyclic Analysis has evolved from Wave Theory. These techniques permit, for the first time, an integrated, self-contained, and completely technical approach to trading and investing in the stock and commodity markets.

The methodology has been field tested since 1971 and is well documented. Computer-generated analysis aids are available.

References

1.	Bachelier, Louis. 1900. *Theory of Speculation. Ann. Sci. Ecole. Norm. Sup.* Vol. 3, No. 1018. Paris: Gauthier-Villars.

2.	Nelson, S.A. 1902. *The ABC of Stock Speculation.* Nelson. Republished 1934. New York: Taylor.

3.	Elliott, R.A. 1939. The Wave Principle, (a series). *Financial World* 90. Also included in: ——. 1946. *Nature's Law.* New York: Elliot.

4.	Hurst, J.M. 1971. *The Profit Magic of Stock Transaction Timing.* Traders Press, Inc. Greenville, SC

5.	*Stock and Commodity Chart Services.* San Francisco: CycliTec Services, 500 Sansome Street.

TRADERS PRESS INC.

Publishers of:
A Complete Guide to Trading Profits (Paris)
A Professional Look at S&P Day Trading (Trivette)
Ask Mr. EasyLanguage (Tennis)
Beginner's Guide to Computer Assisted Trading (Alexander)
Channels and Cycles: A Tribute to J.M. Hurst (Millard)
Chart Reading for Professional Traders (Jenkins)
Commodity Spreads: Analysis, Selection and Trading Techniques (Smith)
Comparison of Twelve Technical Trading Systems (Lukac, Brorsen, & Irwin)
Day Trading with Short Term Price Patterns (Crabel)
Exceptional Trading: The Mind Game (Roosevelt)
Fibonacci Ratios with Pattern Recognition (Pesavento)
Geometry of Stock Market Profits (Jenkins)
Harmonic Vibrations (Pesavento)
How to Trade in Stocks (Livermore)
Hurst Cycles Course (J.M. Hurst)
Jesse Livermore: Speculator King (Sarnoff)
Magic of Moving Averages (Lowry)
Pit Trading: Do You Have the Right Stuff? (Hoffman & Baccetti)
Planetary Harmonics of Speculative Markets (Pesavento)
Point & Figure Charting (Aby)
Point & Figure Charting: Commodity and Stock Trading Techniques (Zieg)
Profitable Grain Trading (Ainsworth)
Profitable Pattern for Stock Trading (Pesavento)
Reminiscences of a Stock Operator (Lefevre)
Stock Market Trading Systems (Appel & Hitschler)
Stock Patterns for Day Trading (Rudd)
Stock Patterns for Day Trading 2 (Rudd)
Study Helps in Point & Figure Techniques (Wheelan)
Technically Speaking (Wilkinson)
Technical Trading Systems for Commodities and Stocks (Patel)
The Professional Commodity Trader (Kroll)
The Taylor Trading Technique (Taylor)
The Traders (Kleinfeld)
*The Trading Rule That Can Make You Rich** (Dobson)
Traders Guide to Technical Analysis (Hardy)
Trading Secrets of the Inner Circle (Goodwin)
Trading S&P Futures and Options (Lloyd)
Understanding Bollinger Bands (Dobson)
Understanding Fibonacci Numbers (Dobson)
Viewpoints of a Commodity Trader (Longstreet)
Wall Street Ventures & Adventures Through Forty Years (Wyckoff)
Winning Market Systems (Appel)

LEGENDARY J.M. HURST CYCLES
TRADING & TRAINING COURSE
AVAILABLE AGAIN FOR THE FIRST
TIME IN A QUARTER OF A CENTURY

The J.M. Hurst Cycles
Trading and Training Course

In the late 1960's, a small group of private investors in California rented time on a mainframe computer—the only kind that existed at that time—and asked an aerospace engineer, J.M. Hurst, to help them in their stock market research. The results of over 20,000 hours of computerized data analysis were distilled and revealed in Hurst's 1970 book, THE PROFIT MAGIC OF STOCK TRANSACTION TIMING, which has become a classic work on cycle analysis.

In the early 1970's, Hurst authored a full-length course on cyclical analysis and on how to apply it to actual trading. It was published by Cyclitech Services, and Hurst taught the principles of this course in a series of seminars for a year or two. The material in this course is considered by many to be the clearest and most thorough material ever made available for those interested in learning about cycles and how to trade profitably with them. There were only 250 copies of the course ever sold. It has been out of print for the past 25 years.

In the mid 1970's, Hurst an intensely private individual, disappeared and has not been heard from again We have had many customers over the years who were tremendously interested in Hurst and his work and were extremely interested in contacting him. They wanted anything he had written or done beyond his PROFIT MAGIC book, but until now, there has been nothing available. I had only heard about this course in "rumor" form for years. Only recently did I actually locate a copy of this course. It had been a dream of mine for years to preserve this curse for posterity and to make it available again to the trading and investing community.

Consisting of ten manuals spanning nearly sixteen hundred pages and eleven full length audio tapes, reproducing it has proven to be an expensive, but exciting and fulfilling challenge. We at Traders Press are proud to make this superb course available once again. It is available exclusively direct from Traders Press.

Edward D. Dobson
President
Traders Press

This course is written by J.M. Hurst, author of THE PROFIT MAGIC OF STOCK TRANSACTION TIMING, a classic work on cyclical analysis. Mr. Hurst is a mathematical analyst who, after 25 years in the aerospace field, spent 30,000 hours researching the nature of stock and commodity price motion.

HERE IS WHAT WELL-KNOWN INVESTMENT
EXPERTS FAMILIAR WITH THE
WORK OF J.M. HURST HAVE TO SAY ABOUT IT

"The work of J.M. Hurst is highly regarded by technical analysts interested in the cyclical approach. Those who want a thorough education on this topic should avail themselves of the opportunity to acquire his full length course, which has been unavailable for many years until recently. The principles it teaches are just as valid today as they were 25 years ago."

—Tim Slater, President, Dow Jones Telerate Seminars

"In the world of channels, bands, and envelopes, J.M. Hurst stands out as a primary source. (THE PROFIT MAGIC OF STOCK TRANSACTION TIMING constitutes the earlier stock-market citation for envelopes I have found.) So it is with great pleasure, and not a little excitement, that I greet 'lost' material from this venerable source. Long out of print and known to but a few, Hurst's course should prove to be an invaluable asset to the research-oriented technical analyst."

—John Bollinger, CFA, CMT

"My copy of "The Profit Magic of Stock Transaction Timing," by J.M. Hurst was only $5.95, when purchased in March of 1979; it remains one of few treasured and frequently referenced volumes. Being an engineer, it is gratifying to find book that us not full of hocus-pocus and magical methods. Hurst's tone clarifies cycles, channels, and brings a host of believable and useful methods for price analysis. Ed Dobson should be 'publisher of the decade' for uncovering and producing a course written by such a major contributor to market analytics. If you have not read his book, you need this course. If you have read his book, you have probably already ordered the course."

—Gregory L. Morris, CEO MURPHYMORRIS, Inc.,
author of *CandlePower and Candlestick Charting Explained*

"Jim Hurst's original cycle work laid the foundation for most of the cycle analysis being done in today's futures and stock markets. The cycle concepts and forecasting techniques are as valid today as they were then. His book and course should be read and studied by all serious students of the markets."

—Walter Bressert, Co-founder of Computrac

"Ever since I read about Hurst's method of 'phasing,' I have looked forward to learning more about his work. His apparently pragmatic approach to technical analysis is very appealing and should adapt well to the more advanced tools now in our hands."

—Perry Kaufman, author of *Commodity Trading Systems and Methods* and numerous other financial titles